LITTLE QUICK FIX: RESEARCH PROPOSAL

#LittleQuickFix

LITTLE QUICK FIX: RESEARCH PROPOSAL

Zina O'Leary

Los Angeles | London | New Delhi
Singapore | Washington DC | Melbourne

Los Angeles | London | New Delhi
Singapore | Washington DC | Melbourne

SAGE Publications Ltd
1 Oliver's Yard
55 City Road
London EC1Y 1SP

SAGE Publications Inc.
2455 Teller Road
Thousand Oaks, California 91320

SAGE Publications India Pvt Ltd
B 1/I 1 Mohan Cooperative Industrial Area
Mathura Road
New Delhi 110 044

SAGE Publications Asia-Pacific Pte Ltd
3 Church Street
#10-04 Samsung Hub
Singapore 049483

Editor: Mila Steele
Editorial assistant: Shelley de Jong
Production editor: Victoria Nicholas
Proofreader: Thea Watson
Marketing manager: Ben Griffin-Sherwood
Design: Shaun Mercier
Typeset by: C&M Digitals (P) Ltd, Chennai, India
Printed in the UK

Library of Congress Control Number: 2018948735

British Library Cataloguing in Publication data

A catalogue record for this book is available from the British Library

ISBN 978-1-5264-5689-2 (pbk)

At SAGE we take sustainability seriously. Most of our products are printed in the UK using responsibly sourced papers and boards. When we print overseas we ensure sustainable papers are used as measured by the PREPS grading system. We undertake an annual audit to monitor our sustainability.

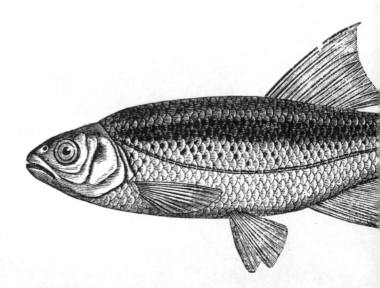

Contents

2 MIN summary

Everything in this book!

Section 1   A research proposal is one of the most important documents you can craft. The proposal 'sells' your project to those in power and covers the merits of the researcher, the research question, and proposed methods.

Section 2   As well as being a critical document for others, a well-considered proposal helps you clarify your thinking, bed down ideas, and articulate thoughts. It is a blueprint for action!

Section 3   In order to write a proposal, you will need to work out a clearly articulated research question and a general research plan. From there, you will need to articulate elements, such as title; abstract; aims/objectives; research question/hypothesis; introduction/background/rationale; literature review; theoretical perspectives; methodology; methods; respondents; limitations/delimitations; ethical considerations; timelines; budget/funding; and references.

Section 4 Writing a winning proposal is about writing purposively while following any guidelines to the letter. Research proposals are often high stakes documents, so be prepared, be logical, and be concise.

Section 5 Obstacles are many, but they are opportunities to hone your thinking. This can happen when: you are forced to challenge your assumptions; your proposed research methods don't fit proposal guidelines; or your methods are evolving or emergent. Being knowledgeable, confident, and open are the keys to getting past them.

Section 6 The DIY workbook at the end of this book is your chance to put your ideas to paper!

Section

The proposal 'sells' your project

What is the purpose of a research proposal?

summary

The research proposal is to be taken seriously!

In fact, it is the gatekeeper for being able to begin or continue your research journey. Its role is to help others assess you and your project's merit. The end game is to get your research off the ground.

Getting a green light

So it's all about getting that green light. In fact, very few research projects get off the ground without some sort of approval. It may be as simple as approval from your lecturer, but it could involve a formal approval process organized through an admissions board, an ethics committee, or a funding body. And, of course, you may need approval from more than one of these. Remember, great ideas are important, but it is the articulation of these ideas that will determine whether you get to cross the start line.

A research proposal is basically a sales pitch. Whether you're after approval from a lecturer, an ethics committee, university admission, or looking for funding, the role of the proposal is to convince the powers that be that what you are proposing meets their requirements. Namely, that the research question, the proposed methods, and the researcher all have merit.

DEMONSTRATING THE MERITS OF YOUR RESEARCH QUESTION

Essential to any successful proposal is selling the merit of your research question. This requires that you:

- clearly and succinctly articulate your research topic and question; and

- demonstrate that your research question is significant enough to warrant support (admission, funding, or ethics approval).

In assessing your question, there are four possibilities:

1   The worth of the research question is self-evident (e.g., 'What are the most effective strategies for curbing cyber bullying?') and you confidently argue the importance and significance of your question.

2   The worth of the research question should be evident, but you do
    a lousy job arguing the case, leaving assessors doubting why you
    were not capable of mounting a straightforward argument.

3   The worth of the research question is not self-evident (e.g., 'Do UK
    residents enjoy watching Dance Mums more than US residents
    enjoy watching Dance Moms?'), but you are able to argue the case
    by citing evidence that attests to a real issue and the benefits of
    conducting relevant research (Good luck with that!).

4   The worth of the research question is not self-evident, and you don't
    help your case. Your arguments are weak, and assessors are left to
    put your proposal in the reject pile.

DEMONSTRATING THE MERITS OF YOUR PROPOSED METHODS

Once assessors are convinced that your research question has merit, their focus will turn to methods. They will be looking to see if proposed methods:

1 **are clearly articulated**. If your assessors cannot make sense of what you're proposing, your proposal has little chance of getting off the ground.

2 **are logical**. Do methods make sense and do the assessors believe your approach can lead to credible data?

3   have taken into consideration **potential hurdles** to effective
    data collection and analysis. Assessors know that all research is
    constrained; your job here is to acknowledge constraints and show
    the credibility of your methods despite any limitations.

4   **are ethical.** Ethics are central to all research processes (and of
    course the main focus of an ethics proposal). Your proposal needs to
    show that the dignity and well-being of respondents, both mentally
    and physically, are fully protected.

5   **are practical/doable.** It doesn't matter how logical and well-
    considered methods are if your assessors don't believe they can
    be implemented. You need to show that: you have or can develop
    necessary expertise; you can gain access to required data; your
    timeline is realistic; and you will come within budget.

DEMONSTRATING THE MERITS OF THE RESEARCHER

Let's assume the assessors are happy with both your question and your methods. The final issue is whether they think you're up to the task. Do they believe you have the necessary background knowledge, at least some familiarity with the literature, and the writing skills to get through?

It would be great if your assessors could get to know you and get a feel for what you are capable of. But that's not likely to happen. In fact, your proposal is likely to be reviewed by people you've never met. So how do they assess potential? Simply on your proposal. Assessors will judge your ability to engage with the literature through your proposal's short literature review. They will assess your ability to carry out method, based on how well you argue your methodological case. And they will assess your potential to write by the quality of writing in your proposal. Attention to detail, therefore, counts. Your proposal needs to be one of the tightest pieces of writing you have ever attempted.

Got it?

Q: What are the three things you need to do in your proposal to demonstrate that you are ready to undertake your research?

Got it!

A:

1 Be able to sell the merits of your research question

2 Be able to sell the robustness and integrity of your methodological design

3 Be able to sell yourself as a capable researcher

A research proposal is a blueprint for action!

2

Section

How can I get the most benefit out of writing a research proposal?

Think about questions. Think about design. Think about logistics.

Grab the opportunity!

Your proposal may be a critical document for outsiders, but it is also your opportunity to get to grips with your research project. So while you may be writing this for others, also make sure you are writing this for yourself. What you are working on is not just another paper. It is not just administrative. It is, in fact, your blueprint for action.

Coming up with a research question and an accompanying research design is no simple task. It is easy to become totally stuck or be overwhelmed with too many ideas. Crafting a research proposal offers you a huge opportunity – actually one of two opportunities. The first is if you are completely stuck and your brain feels like an empty vessel, the requirement of crafting a proposal will force you to come up with something! On the flipside, your issue might be too many ideas. You know, ideas that afflict your brain, but never quite solidify into a workable project. In either case, it is time. If there is one thing about proposals, it's that deadlines are firm. Proposals have a way of stopping procrastination dead in its tracks.

Your mind is a blank and you need some inspiration. Well, there are some steps you can take:

1 review project criteria – this is so you have a good idea of your target;

2 write down a potential list of broad topics that might suit criteria – this can be as broad as media, economy, health, bullying, climate, etc;

3 pick one of these areas that is of particular interest.

IF YOU ARE STUCK WITHOUT ANY GOOD IDEAS

4 Explore the topic by asking:

- what issues surround this?

- are there any obvious needs?

- does anything in this area frustrate you or members of the community?

- is there anything in the media that might clue you in to issues?

- what do others think is interesting about this topic?

5 Try mind mapping your answers – I bet you come up with a few workable ideas.

What if you have too many ideas? Well, if this is your issue, it's not so bad. Ideas are great. But when one idea follows another, nothing settles, and you just can't take anything to an endpoint, well, you're not really getting anywhere.

If this is your tendency – know that it's okay. Ideas are essential, so it is not about stemming them, it is about harnessing them. Here are some tips:

1 write down all your ideas – if you are going to assess them, you need to capture them

2 define and write down criteria for a 'good idea'. This might include:
   appropriateness of topic; ability to collect relevant data; will get
   through ethics processes; is the right timeframe; in my interest; is of
   some significance, etc.

3 for each idea, assess how each meets your criteria

4 commit to the ideas that fit your criteria best

5 commit to working it up to a completed proposal.

IF YOU HAVE TOO MANY IDEAS

Try a
mind map

Example:

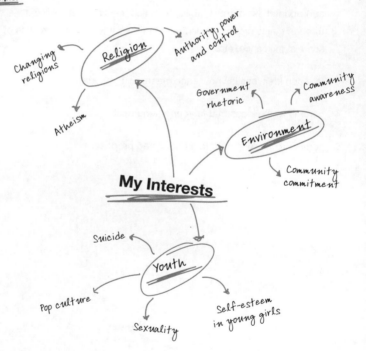

Changing religions

Religion

Authority, power and control

Atheism

Government rhetoric

Community awareness

Environment

Community commitment

My Interests

Suicide

Youth

Pop culture

Sexuality

Self-esteem in young girls

Start with the right idea

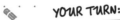

YOUR TURN:

Start with your research topic in the centre, work out towards broad topics, and in the clouds explore the issues related to this topic

TOO MANY IDEAS?

Assess with a flow chart

Work each idea through the following:

YOUR IDEA

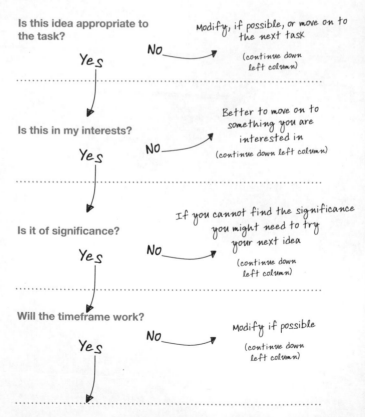

Is this idea appropriate to the task?

Yes

NO → Modify, if possible, or move on to the next task

(continue down left column)

Is this in my interests?

Yes

NO → Better to move on to something you are interested in

(continue down left column)

Is it of significance?

Yes

NO → If you cannot find the significance you might need to try your next idea

(continue down left column)

Will the timeframe work?

Yes

NO → Modify if possible

(continue down left column)

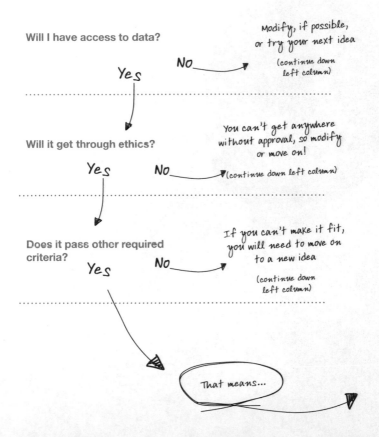

Will I have access to data?

Modify, if possible, or try your next idea

(continue down left column)

Yes

NO

Will it get through ethics?

You can't get anywhere without approval, so modify or move on!

(continue down left column)

Yes

NO

Does it pass other required criteria?

If you can't make it fit, you will need to move on to a new idea

(continue down left column)

Yes

NO

That means...

Write your core research idea here:

_____

You will need to work
out a clearly articulated
research question and a
general research plan

Section

What do I need to work out before I start writing the proposal?

summary

First, you will need to be familiar with all the required sections of the proposal. Second, you will need to know all the parameters of your project: question, methods, and everything else.

It's all in the preparation!

When it comes to this research project, just how well developed is your thinking? Is your question clear and well-articulated? Have you defined methods? Have you thought through respondents and ethics? What about data collection and analysis? If you have a question mark next to these items, it is time to think it through and bed it down. Almost as important is knowing that proposal form. Understand it. Become familiar with its ins and outs. Understand what it is asking of you. The more you can get your head around what is being asked of you, the better off you'll be.

KNOW YOUR STUFF

When it comes to preparing to complete your research proposal, you need to know what you want to know. This is where it starts – with a well-articulated research question. Research is all about getting the answers to a question – and your proposal is about articulating the steps you will take to get to the answer. If you are struggling with this, it might be worth checking out *Little Quick Fix: Research Question*. This is the single most important thing to nail when getting ready to make a start.

Once you have your question, you need to know how you will get answers.

- What is the context of your study? (Background information is essential.)

- What have other researchers found? (This will be the basis of your literature review.)

- Where do your answers lie? (This will point you to methods.)

- Who are your potential respondents, are any from marginalized groups, and how will you recruit them? (Extremely important for an ethics proposal.)

- What are your proposed methods? (This is the nitty gritty of data collection and analysis.) Are there ethical implications? (These are not always obvious and must be thought through.)

- What about costs? (Both time and money.) Will you finish on time? (Committees always want to insure you can complete in good time.)

Once you have the answers to all the above, the next step is to understand how this planning maps to the required elements of the research proposal. Generally, elements of a proposal cover some combination of the following:

- title
- abstract
- aims/objectives
- research question/hypothesis
- introduction/background/rationale
- literature review
- theoretical perspectives
- methodology
- methods
- respondents
- limitations/delimitations
- ethical considerations
- timelines
- budget/funding, and
- references

Jackpot

THE 'ARE YOU READY?' CHECKLIST

Going through this checklist will let you know exactly where you need to continue your proposal prep

Do you have a clear and well-articulated research question?	Yes / No
Are your aim and objectives clear?	Yes / No
Are you familiar with the body of literature related to this area?	Yes / No
Can you articulate the context for your study?	Yes / No
Are you referencing any theory?	Yes / No
Have you defined your overarching methodology?	Yes / No
Do you know where you can access relevant data?	Yes / No
If this is desk research, do you know what documents, websites, etc. you need to access?	Yes / No
If you are working with respondents, do you have a recruitment plan?	Yes / No

CHECKPOINT

Do you have a plan for protecting the interests of respondents?   Yes / No

Have you determined how you will get data from your respondents?   Yes / No

Do you know how you will analyse your data?   Yes / No

Are you aware of any shortcomings in your methods?   Yes / No

Do you have a timeline?   Yes / No

Have you considered any financial costs of your research?   Yes / No

Do you have references ready?   Yes / No

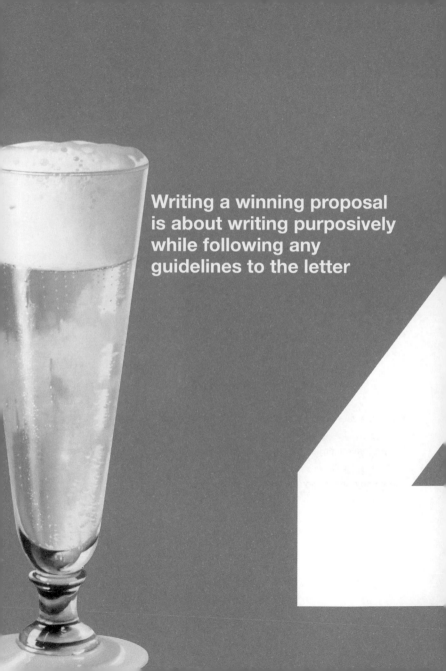

Writing a winning proposal is about writing purposively while following any guidelines to the letter

4

Section

1

How can I write so that my proposal is a winner?

summary

Writing a winning
proposal involves two
main things. The first
is to be able to clearly
articulate the dimensions
of your research that
were highlighted in
the last section –
communication is key.
The second is following
guidelines – pedantically.

Write like it counts!

Because it does. The proposal is all there is. Generally speaking, it is all
that assessors have to make a decision about your future. They aren't
able to wander through your mind; they won't know if you're planning
to work on a long-standing passion; they won't know that you're better
in action then on paper. In short, they probably don't know much about
you and your capability, except for what's in your proposal.

So, you need to make sure this document sells you like no other. The
best advice here? Write, rewrite, draft, redraft until you are giving them
exactly what they asked for. And finally, don't go it alone; get plenty of
feedback!

CLEARLY ARTICULATING WHAT YOU KNOW

Writing up a proposal is no easy task. The **following steps** will make it more systematic and easier to manage.

1 **Get access to a few successful proposals** Seek out proposals that have gone through the committee (or lecturer) you are applying to, or to as similar a committee as possible – these might be online. If not, Google 'research proposal example' and your level and area of study. Keep in mind, however, that not all proposals on the Internet are good ones!

2 **Find a voice** Third person is conventional, however, using 'I' to state what you will do is now more commonly accepted. Also, remember to write in the future tense. A proposal is about what you will do, not what you are doing now, or have done in the past.

3 'Write tight' Be concise and succinct, direct and straightforward. Avoid rambling and/or trying to show off by using unnecessary jargon.

4 Write enough Somewhat paradoxical to the above, you also need to make sure you write a sufficient amount for assessors to make judgements.

5 Write for the 'non-expert' Your proposal needs to be 'stand-alone' and comprehensible to someone potentially outside your field.

6 **Do your homework** Get your facts right, make sure you don't have gaping holes in your literature, and make sure any references to theory and/or methods are accurate.

7 **Don't over quote** With tight word counts, you probably won't have enough room for too many direct quotes. Keep the words and ideas yours, supported by the literature.

8 Draft and redraft The advice here is write, rewrite, and rewrite some more. And once you are done, check it against both an expert who can help you assess if your application is appropriate for the field and a non-expert who can let you know if it is logical for the lay person.

9 Don't let the deadline sneak up on you Finish early so that you have time for all contingencies. Remember: deadlines are generally inflexible.

THE 'GET PREPARED' CHECKLIST!

☐ Do you have a copy of the proposal template?

☐ Have you accessed previous proposals?

☐ Have you attempted a rough draft of the template?

☐ Have you identified any gaps arising from this first attempt?

☐ Have you discussed any sticking points with your supervisor/lecturer?

Make sure you can check off all five

A LITTLE QUICK
STYLE GUIDE

✓ Be clear, fluent, and logical

✓ Use a consistent voice

✓ Make your point with convincing arguments

✓ Include sufficient information, but avoid repetition, waffling, and paragraph-long sentences

✓ Limit acronyms and jargon

✓ Have exemplary spelling and grammar and avoid all typos

✓ Be well-formatted

FOLLOWING GUIDELINES

Assessors tend to want what they want… the way they want it… when they want it. This means you need to be just as pedantic and make sure you follow all guidelines. So just how many words can you get away with when the application says the title needs to be no more than 20 words or that the abstract must be less than 150 words? Well, I certainly wouldn't stretch it. Some assessors can judge harshly when they think applicants cannot follow simple directions. Remember – applications can be seen as a test of whether you will be able to meet requirements when you actually start working on your project. The thinking here is that if you cannot follow guidelines in a short application, you might struggle to complete.

The research proposal pedant's <u>FOUR RULES</u>

Construct your proposal according to, or as close as possible to, the recommended section/headings. Be a pedant!

Don't go any further until you pass these four rules

1   Keep to all word limits

2   Fill in every section

3   Include any additional requested documents

4   Strictly adhere to deadlines

Section

5

Obstacles are opportunities to hone your thinking

What can go wrong and how do I overcome obstacles?

summary

You probably know that
things going to plan is
more of an exception
than a rule, and this is
certainly true of research
proposals. Remember,
a proposal does not just
capture where you are...
it's actually a process
that is likely to evolve
your thinking... and that
evolution is a challenge
in itself.

It's a process!

Challenges… well there are several. But remember, this is a process and even if you find it challenging, you will get there. Now you may find yourself overwhelmed at having to make definitive decisions. Or, you might struggle to coherently and logically share those decisions with others. The process of writing may see you identify: holes in your logic; flaws in your methodology; or ethical challenges. So don't be surprised if you find yourself in a bit of a tangle. But this isn't a bad thing. Research logic is tricky and grappling with it at this stage is a healthy, albeit frustrating, part of the process.

Even after you have worked out the logic and all your initial methodological challenges, there are still obstacles you might face. For example, you may need to navigate a research design that doesn't neatly fit proposal requirements or you may have an emergent design that is hard to capture.

WHEN YOU REALIZE THAT YOUR METHODOLOGY ISN'T QUITE WHERE YOU WANT IT

Do not be surprised if this process causes you to challenge your own thinking and assumptions. The best advice here is to rigorously assess your own logic and processes. Earlier, you checked off elements of your design. Now, it is time to challenge them. Ask yourself:

- Are you happy with your research question? Is it precisely what you want to know?

- If you are carrying out 'desk' research, can the documents you access credibly and rigorously answer your research question?

- What is your population (the range of people you want your study to speak for)?

Struggling with these questions will evolve your project in the right direction

- What is your sample, and does it adequately represent your population?

- Are your strategies for accessing this sample practical and ethical?

- Are there any potential ethical issues in your data collection protocol?

- Will respondents open up to you and be truthful?

- Are you sure that your protocols will allow you to gather credible data that will adequately answer your research question?

WHEN YOUR DESIGN DOES NOT FIT PROPOSAL REQUIREMENTS

The advice so far has been to give assessors precisely what they ask for. But sometimes your design does not fit committee requirements. This can be the case in 'qualitative' research where hypothesis, variables, validity, and reliability may be referenced in the application, but not be appropriate to your study.

Seek the advice here of someone in the know. You are unlikely to be the first to come across this dilemma. If you can't get insider information, remember the bigger picture: that proposals need to demonstrate the merits of the research question, the proposed methods, and the researcher. Regardless of paradigm, you need to be confident with the conceptual and methodological landscape you're proposing. So, write confidently… but not aggressively nor apologetically. Any assessor worth his/her weight will be able to spot a researcher who knows what he or she is talking about, even when it doesn't fit with the committee's expectations/jargon.

WHEN YOUR DESIGN IS EMERGENT

Perhaps you're proposing a study with evolving methods; methods that can't be fully articulated when the proposal is due. Ethics proposals, for example, often demand a full account of methods, including surveys and interview schedules. If your proposal includes conversational, unstructured, or not fully determined data-gathering techniques, this can pose a challenge. Action research, conducted in evolving cycles, is also emergent. In fact, there are many research projects with multiple phases, with each phase determined by what has happened previously, i.e., interviews may be used to inform survey design, or survey results may determine the questions used in in-depth interviewing.

The best strategy here is to be open and knowledgeable about your approach. Show that your design is not haphazard or ill-considered. Even if you cannot articulate all the specifics, your required flexibility is planned and sits within a defined framework. Offer, if possible, indicative questions. And finally, show that you can link your approach back to accepted methodological literature.

If assessors still require further information you have three options: 1) add more definition and details; 2) see if you can put in a supplementary application as your methods progress; or 3) talk to your supervisor about modifying your design.

Time to digest

Grab your pen and answer the following questions

Are you confident with the logic and methods of your proposal? If not, what needs to change?

Now that you've considered any potential changes, ask yourself:

Does your proposal fit neatly into the proposal requirements/template? If not, what strategies will you use to give the committee what they require, while staying true to your design/paradigm?

Solved that one? Great, now time to think about design

Is your design emergent? If so, how can you articulate the logic of this approach?

If there are any questions you don't feel you answered with confidence, give it another go. You'll get there

SECTION

6

Put your ideas to paper!
The DIY workbook

What is the best way to attack my proposal?

summary

By doing!

Time to do it!

This workbook section covers all sections likely to be required in your proposal. It offers an explanation of each section, an example, and space for you to write up a few of your own notes (it might be old school, but putting actual pen to actual paper can absolutely get the brain firing). In fact, think of this workbook as your own personal research proposal builder!

Keep in mind that proposal requirements vary by committee and type of approval you're seeking. So have a look at your particular requirements (including word counts) and open up their template or start a purpose-built Word document. You might as well use your notes to make a start.

YOUR
WORKBOOK

Open a file to start building your research proposal and hit 'save'. There is space here to scribble down a few guiding ideas for your research proposal. First stop: the title.

TITLE

What to do: Go for clear, concise, and unambiguous. Your title should indicate the specific content and context of the problem you wish to explore in as succinct a way as possible.

YOUR TURN:

Can you come up with a clear title?

ABSTRACT

What to do: Proposals often require an abstract, usually with a very tight word count. The trick here is to briefly state the what, why, and how of your project in a way that captures its significance.

Example: This study will use a case study approach to identify the types of images university students post and will seek to determine if user characteristics vary according to the primary types of images posted. A random sample of 100 Instagram accounts from students at the University of X will be analyzed using a grounded theory approach used to create a taxonomy of image types. Users will then be identified by the primary type of images they post, and they will then be correlated to user characteristics, such as gender, age, degree, and extracurricular activities.

YOUR TURN:

Jot down a few points that capture the gist of your project

AIMS/ OBJECTIVES

What to do: Most proposals have one overarching aim that captures what you hope to achieve through your project. A set of objectives, which are more specific goals, supports that aim.

YOUR TURN:

Rewrite your research idea as an aim, and add a few working objectives

RESEARCH QUESTION/ HYPOTHESIS

What to do: A concise well-articulated research question is essential. Any committee reviewing your proposal will turn to your question to get an overall sense of your project.

A hypothesis is a logical conjecture about the nature of relationships between two or more variables expressed in the form of a testable statement. It is only applicable for studies that are testing the relationship between variables.

Example: What types of images do university students post on Instagram and do their characteristics vary based on the types of images they post?

YOUR TURN:

Write down a question that captures your key terms with precision. Ensure there is a tight logic

INTRODUCTION/ BACKGROUND/ RATIONALE

What to do: This section introduces your topic and convinces readers that the problem you want to address is significant, worth exploring, and even funding. It should give some context to the problem and lead your readers to the conclusion that, yes, research into this area is absolutely essential if we want to work towards situation improvement or problem resolution.

Example: The photo sharing application, Instagram, has become a cultural phenomenon, particularly among millennials. In fact, 59% of 18 to 24 year olds are active on the social platform. However, as a relatively new application, research into this form of social connection is in its infancy. This study will contribute to understanding what a key group of users, university students, are posting on Instagram and how this varies by various types of students. The goal is to garner preliminary insights into the online social world of students as offered through their own lenses and lay the groundwork for further study.

YOUR TURN:

Jot down key points that will help you argue the significance of your project

LITERATURE REVIEW

What to do: A formal 'literature review' is a specific piece of argumentative writing that engages with academic research in order to create a space for your research. The literature review informs readers of the field while establishing your own credibility as a person capable of adding to this body of knowledge.

Example: Since its launch in October 2010, Instagram has attracted more than 800 million active users, with an average of over 100 million photos uploaded every day (Instagram 2018). Despite these statistics, studies into Instagram's use and cultural meaning are in an early stage (Hu, Manikonda, and Kambhampati 2014). Investigations that have taken place tend to focus on demographics and composition (Pittman and Reich B 2016). Yet, Instagram as compared to any other social media platform corroborates the recent Pew report that highlights how photos and videos have become the key social currencies online (Rainie, Brenner, and Purcell 2012).

YOUR TURN:

Start a list of relevant literature here.
u can then go back to your research proposal
file to start to construct arguments

THEORETICAL PERSPECTIVES

What to do: This section asks you to situate your study in a conceptual or theoretical framework. The idea here is to articulate the theoretical perspective(s) that underpin and inform your ideas, and, in particular, to discuss how 'theory' relates to and/or directs your study.

Example: The theoretical perspective that informs this project is narrative theory. Narrative theory explores the production, practices, and communication of storytelling accounts (Bell 2002). Gubrium and Holstein's work on the interplay of everyday storytelling and larger cultural discourses (2009) will provide the context for understanding how images create a particular presentation of self (Goffman 1959).

YOUR TURN:

What theories support your work?

METHODS

Some form of 'methods' will be required in all proposals. The goal here is to articulate your plan with enough clarity and detail to convince readers that your approach is practical/ethical and will lead to credible answers to the questions posed. Under the heading of methods, you would generally articulate your **methodology**.

What it is: Frameworks that offer principles of reasoning associated with particular paradigmatic assumptions. For example, if you are doing ethnography, action research, or maybe a randomized controlled trial.

Example: This study will use a mixed methodology. The taxonomy of image types will use qualitative image analysis through a grounded theory approach. A quantitative approach will be used to analyse preliminary surveys and to compare identified user types.

YOUR TURN:

Jot down notes on your methodological approach

RESPONDENTS

What it is: This includes stating population and sample as well as sampling procedures. Ethics committees will be very focused on how you recruit your sample and that potential respondents are fully informed of all processes, as well as their right to discontinue. You will also need to take care if proposing the study of marginalized groups (children, minorities, etc.). They will want assurance that these groups are not being singled out for study in ways that exploit.

Example: The researcher will ask students taking introductory sociology courses at the University of X to participate in a voluntary study analyzing their Instagram accounts. Students will be given an explanatory statement outlining the full nature of the study and will be offered the right to discontinue at any time. Only students 18 years and older will be allowed to participate.

YOUR TURN:

Note your sample and your plans for recruitment

METHODS OF DATA COLLECTION

What it is: This includes data collection protocols, such as surveying, interviewing, and document analysis.

Example: Data collection will consist of: 1) a preliminary survey of the 100 participants; 2) content analysis of images on the participants' Instagram accounts.

YOUR TURN:

Note all forms of data collection you will be using

METHODS OF ANALYSIS

What it is: Whether you will be doing statistical or thematic analysis and perhaps variants thereof.

Example: Data analysis will consist of: 1) descriptive statistics from preliminary surveys generated using SPSS; 2) a grounded theory approach to the analysis of Instagram images; 3) inferential statistics correlating types of image posted and other user demographic characteristics using SPSS.

YOUR TURN:

Note all forms of analysis you will be using

DELIMITATIONS/ LIMITATIONS

What it is: Delimitations refer to a study's boundaries or how your study was deliberately narrowed by conscious exclusions and inclusions, e.g., delimiting your study to children of a certain age only or schools from one particular region. **Limitations** refer to design characteristics of your study that may impact the generalizability and utility of findings, such as small sample size or restricted access to records. Keep in mind that most projects are limited by constraints, such as time, resources, access, or organizational issues. Remember that your goal here is to convince readers that your findings will be credible despite any limitations or delimitations. So, the trick is to be open about your study's parameters without sounding defensive or apologetic. It is also worth articulating any strategies you will be using to ensure credibility despite limitations.

Example: Delimitations: this study is delimited to university students, a key user group of Instagram. Limitations: this study will rely on a small sample size at one particular university and be limited to introductory sociology students. Its generalizability will, therefore, be limited. The study, however, will provide valuable insights into how this particular group of university students uses Instagram and will offer valuable insights for further research.

YOUR TURN:

Think through your study and make notes on its parameters

ETHICAL CONSIDERATIONS

What this means: If you are working with human participants you will need to consider ethics. In an ethics application you would need to focus much of your proposal on ethical issues. But even in an admission or funding proposal, you would still need to convince assessors that you have considered integrity in the production of knowledge and responsibility for the emotional, physical, and intellectual well-being of your study participants.

Example: Participation in this study is voluntary and limited to those 18 years and older. All participants will be given a full explanatory statement. Results will be aggregated, and no personal information will be made public. Participants will be made aware of their right to discontinue at any time.

YOUR TURN:

List the ethical considerations important to your work

TIMELINE

What it is: This is simply superimposing a timeline on your methods, and is often done in a tabular or chart form. The committee reading your proposal will be looking to see that your plan is realistic and can conform to any overarching timeframes or deadlines.

Example:

ACTIVITY	% Complete	Jan	Feb	Mar	Apr	May	Jun	Jul	Aug	Sep	Oct	Nov	Dec
Question Development	100%	▨	▨	▨									
Method Development	100%			▨	▨								
Proposal	100%				▨								
Literature Review	25%	▨	▨	▨	▨	▨	▨	▨	▨	▨	▨		
Participant Recruitment	0%					▨							
Survey	0%						▨						
Taxonomy Development	0%						▨	▨	▨				
Identification of User Type	0%								▨				
Correlations	0%									▨			
Writing Up	0%			▨		▨	▨	▨	▨	▨	▨	▨	▨
Presentation	0%												
Submission	0%												

YOUR TURN:

Make some notes on your timeline activities here, but this is actually a good thing to work up on Excel afterwards

ACTIVITY	% Complete	Jan	Feb	Mar	Apr	May	Jun	Jul	Aug	Sep	Oct	Nov	Dec

BUDGET/FUNDING

What this means: This is a full account of costs and who will bear them. While not always a required section for ethics proposals or proposals for academic student research, it will certainly be a requirement for a funding body.

Example: The costs for this project will be photocopying and printing which will be covered by the sociology department. The department has also agreed to fund a £150 dinner voucher as a prize to encourage survey participation.

YOUR TURN:

Write down any costs you foresee and how they will be met

REFERENCES

What this means: This can refer to two things. The first is citing references in the same way as you would in any other type of academic/professional writing. Believe it or not, this is often missed. The second is that some committees want a list of, say, 10 or 15 primary references that will inform your work. This information can help a committee assess your knowledge and get a clearer indication of the direction your study may take.

One more task! Last but not least...

Example:

REFERENCES

Aslan, S. (2018) *Instagram by the Numbers: Stats, Demographics & Fun Facts...* Omnicore. Retrieved from www.omnicoreagency.com/instagram-statistics.

Bell, J. S. (2002) 'Narrative inquiry: More than just telling stories...' *TESOL Quarterly*, 36 (2), 207–213.

And so on...

YOUR TURN:

Start by jotting your reference list here, and then it would be beneficial to use a referencing software, such as EndNote or BibMe

CONGRATULATIONS! YOU'VE DONE IT

YOU SHOULD NOW
BE IN A TERRIFIC
POSITION TO KICK THAT
PROPOSAL INTO GEAR

Time now to make a
commitment!

I will submit my proposal on

_____

_____ / _____ / _____

#LittleQuickFix

To help ensure you have mastered all you need to know to write a winning research proposal, work through this checklist

☐ Do you understand the importance of the research proposal and how it can 'sell' you and your project? If not, go back to p. 7

☐ Are you able to use the proposal process as a means for pushing your conceptual thinking along? If not, go back to p. 21

☐ Have you been able to capture all your thinking related to the key elements of your proposal? If not, go back to p. 37

HOW TO KNOW YOU ARE DONE

☐ Are you prepared to write purposively and succinctly while following all guidelines? If not, go back to p. 49

☐ Have you challenged your own assumptions and checked the logic of everything you are proposing? If not, go back to p. 63

☐ Have you attempted (even better, completed!) relevant sections of the workbook? If not, definitely go back to p. 75

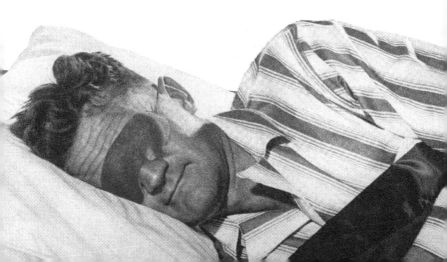

Glossary

Abstract A synopsis of your research processes.

Action research Research strategies that tackle real-world problems in participatory and collaborative ways in multiple cycles.

Aims and objectives An aim is what you hope to achieve through your research project – generally a restatement of the research question. Objectives are the stepwise achievements expected in the study that will help you reach your aim.

Broad representation Representation wide enough to ensure that a targeted institution, cultural group, or phenomenon can be spoken about confidently.

Delimitations A study's boundaries, for example conscious exclusions in your defined population.

Ethics Refers to a professional 'code of practice' designed to protect the researched from an unethical process, and in turn protect the researcher from legal liabilities.

Grounded theory A form of qualitative data analysis that uses inductive processes to generate theory directly from data.

Hypothesis Logical conjecture about the nature of relationships between two or more variables expressed in the form of a testable statement.

Limitations Design characteristics or constraints that may have an impact on the generalizability and utility of findings, for example small sample size or restricted access to records.

Literature review A critical and purposive review of a body of knowledge including findings and theoretical and methodological contributions.

Methodology Macro-level frameworks that offer principles of reasoning associated with particular assumptions. Examples here include scientific method, ethnography, and action research.

Methods The actual micro-level techniques used to collect and analyse data.

Paradigm A worldview that underpins the theories and methodology of a particular discipline or scientific subject.

Respondents Individuals who agree to provide data for your research project.

Qualitative approach An approach to research highly reliant on qualitative data (words, images, experiences, and observations that are not quantified).

Quantitative approach An approach to research highly reliant on quantified data (numerical data as well as concepts we code with numbers).

Sample A subset of a population.

Theoretical perspectives A set of assumptions about reality that informs the questions we ask and the kinds of answers we seek.

Variables Constructs that have more than one value; variables can be 'hard' (e.g., gender, height, or income) or 'soft' (e.g., self-esteem, worth, or political opinion).